TELEPHONE RINGING
IN THE
LABYRINTH

TELEPHONE RINGING IN THE LABYRINTH

POEMS
2004–2006

ADRIENNE RICH

W. W. Norton & Company
New York • London

Copyright © 2007 by Adrienne Rich

Manufacturing by Courier Westford
Book design by Charlotte Staub
Production manager: Anna Oler

Library of Congress Cataloging-in-Publication Data

Rich, Adrienne Cecile.
Telephone ringing in the labyrinth : poems, 2004–2006 / Adrienne Rich. — 1st ed.
p. cm.
Includes bibliographical references.
ISBN 978-0-393-06565-7
I. Title.
PS3535.I233T45 2007
811'.54—dc22   2007023235

W. W. Norton & Company, Inc.
500 Fifth Avenue, New York, N.Y. 10110
www.wwnorton.com

W. W. Norton & Company Ltd.
Castle House, 75/76 Wells Street, London W1T 3QT

1 2 3 4 5 6 7 8 9 0

Poetry isn't easy to come by.
You have to write it like you owe a debt to the world.
In that way poetry is how the world comes to be in you.

—ALAN DAVIES

Poetry is not self-expresssion, the I is a dramatic I.

—MICHAEL S. HARPER,
QUOTING STERLING A. BROWN

To which I would add: and so, unless
otherwise indicated, is the You.

—A.R.

CONTENTS

I

II

TELEPHONE RINGING
IN THE
LABYRINTH

I

VOYAGE TO THE DENOUEMENT

A child's hand smears a wall   the reproof is bitter
    wall contrives to linger   child, punisher, gone in smoke
An artisan lays on hues: lemon, saffron, gold
    stare hard before you start covering the whole room
Inside the thigh a sweet mole   on the balding
    skull an irregular island   what comes next
After the burnt forests   silhouettes wade
    liquid hibiscus air
Velvet rubs down to scrim   iron utensils
    discolor unseasoned
Secret codes of skin and hair
    go dim   left from the light too long

Because my wish was to have things simpler
    than they were   memory too became
a smudge   sediment from a hand
    repeatedly lying on the same surface
Call it a willful optimism
    from when old ownerships unpeeled   curled out
into the still nameless   new imperium   Call it
    haplessness of a creature   not yet ready
for her world-citizen's papers
    (Across the schoolroom mural   bravely
small ships did under sail traverse great oceans)
    Rain rededicates the exhumed
African burial ground
    traffic lashes its edges

the city a scar a fragment floating
    on tidal dissolution
The opal on my finger
    fiercely flashed till the hour it started to crumble

2004

CALIBRATIONS

She tunes her guitar for Landstuhl
where she will sit on beds and sing
ballads from when Romany
roamed Spain

. . .

A prosthetic hand calibrates perfectly
the stem of a glass
or how to stroke a face
is this how far we have come
to make love easy

Ghost limbs go into spasm in the night
You come back from war with the body you have

. . .

What you can't bear
carry endure lift
you'll have to drag

it'll come with you the ghostlimb

the shadow   blind
echo of your body spectre of your soul

. . .

Let's not talk yet of making love
nor of ingenious devices
replacing touch

And this is not theoretical:
A poem with calipers to hold a heart
so it will want to go on beating

2004

SKELETON KEY

In the marina an allegro creaking
boats on the tide
each with its own sway
                                    rise and fall
acceptance and refusal
La Barqueta, My Pelican

barometer in the body
rising and falling

. . .

A small wound, swallow-shaped, on my wrist
ripped by a thorn
exacerbated by ash and salt

And this is how I came to be
protector of the private
and enemy of the personal

. . .

Then I slept, and had a dream
No more
No màs

From now on, only
reason's drugged and dreamless sleep

. . .

Creeps down the rockface   shadow cast
from an opposite crag exactly at that moment
you needed light on the trail   These are the shortening days
you forgot about   bent on your own design

. . .

Cut me a skeleton key
to that other time, that city
talk starting up, deals and poetry

Tense with elation, exiles
walking old neighborhoods
calm journeys of streetcars

revived boldness of cats
locked eyes of couples
music playing full blast again

Exhuming the dead   Their questions

2004

WALLPAPER

1

A room papered with clippings:
newsprint in bulging patches
none of them mentions our names
gone from that history then   O red

kite snarled in a cloud
small plane melted in fog: no matter:
I worked to keep it current
and meaningful: a job of living I thought

history as wallpaper
urgently selected clipped and pasted
but the room itself   nowhere

gone the address   the house
golden-oak banisters zigzagging
upward, stained glass on the landings
streaked porcelain in the bathrooms

loose floorboards quitting in haste we pried
up to secrete the rash imagination
of a time to come

What we said then, our breath   remains
otherwhere: in me   in you

2

Sonata for Unaccompanied Minor
Fugitive Variations
discs we played over and over

on the one-armed phonograph
Childish we were in our adoration
of the dead composer

who'd ignored the weather signs
trying to cross the Andes
stupidly   I'd say now

and you'd agree   seasoned
as we are   working stretched
weeks   eating food bought

with ordinary grudging wages
keeping up with rent, utilities

a job of living as I said

3

Clocks are set back   quick dark
snow filters past my lashes
this is the common ground

white-crusted sidewalks   windshield wipers
licking, creaking
to and *fro*   *to* and *fro*

If the word gets out if the word
escapes if the word
flies if it dies
it has its way of coming back

The handwritings on the walls
are vast and coded

the music blizzards past

2004

IN PLAIN SIGHT

My neighbor moving
in a doorframe   moment's
reach of her hand   then

withdrawn   As from some old
                        guilty pleasure

Smile etched like a scar
which must be borne
                        Smile
in a photograph taken against one's will

Her son up on a ladder stringing
along the gutter
electric icicles in a temperate zone

If the suffering hidden in plain sight
is of her past her future
or the thin-ice present where
we're balancing here
                        or how she sees it
I can't presume

. . . Ice-thin.   Cold and precarious
the land I live in and have argued not to leave
Cold on the verge of crease
                        crack without notice

ice-green disjuncture   treasoning us
to flounder cursing each other
Cold and grotesque the sex
the grimaces the grab

A *privilege*   you say
to live here   A *luxury*
Everyone still wants to come here!
You want a christmas card, a greeting
to tide us over
with pictures of the children

then you demand a valentine
an easterlily   anything for the grab
a mothersday menu   wedding invitation

It's not as in a museum that I
observe
and mark in every Face I meet

            under crazed surfaces
traces of feeling   locked in shadow

Not as in a museum of history
do I pace here   nor as one who in a show
of bland paintings shrugs and walks on   I gaze
through faces   not as an X-ray
                              nor
as paparazzo shooting
the compromised celebrity

nor archaeologist filming
the looted site
nor as the lover tearing out of its frame
the snapshot to be held to a flame

but as if a mirror
forced to reflect a room
                    the figures

standing   the figures crouching

2004

BEHIND THE MOTEL

A man lies under a car half bare
a child plays bullfight with a torn cloth
hemlocks grieve in wraps of mist
a woman talks on the phone, looks in a mirror
fiddling with the metal pull of a drawer

She has seen her world wiped clean, the cloth
that wiped it disintegrate in mist
or dying breath on the skin of a mirror
She has felt her life close like a drawer
has awoken somewhere else, bare

He feels his skin as if it were mist
as if his face would show in no mirror
He needs some bolts he left in a vanished drawer
crawls out into the hemlocked world with his bare
hands, wipes his wrench on an oil-soaked cloth

stares at the woman talking into a mirror
who has shut the phone into the drawer
while over and over with a torn cloth
at the edge of hemlocks behind the bare
motel a child taunts a horned beast made from mist

2004

PIANO MÉLANCOLIQUE (extraits)

par Élise Turcotte

N'emporte rien avec toi.
Essayons de croire
qu'il n'y a rien dans mes poumons.
Qu'aucune maladie ne noircit
tes yeux.
Que je t'écris de la mangrove
pour te parler des palétuviers
qui sont les personnages
les plus mystérieux que j'aie vu.

Fantomatique, comme les
arbres, je reviens aux paysages.

Vapeurs et reflets.
Et petites racines aériennes
fixées au bas de ma robe.

MELANCHOLY PIANO (extracts)

from the French of Élise Turcotte

Take nothing with you.
Let's try believing
there's nothing in my lungs.
That no sickness clouds
your eyes.
That I write you from the swamp
to tell you about the mangroves
the most mysterious
presences I've seen.

Spectral as the
trees, I return to landscape.

Fumes and reflections.
And little airy roots
stuck to the hem of my skirt.

Je me décris comme un animal
à plumes.
Je décris. Tu regardes.
Tandis que poussent mes plumes.

La nuit, tu cherches un motif fragile,
un relief aussi précis qu'un visage
aimé.

Des insectes occupent la chapelle cachée
sous le sable.

Beaucoup d'années ont passé
jusqu'ici.

I describe myself as a feathered
animal.
I describe.   You watch.
While my plumes grow.

Nights, you search for a fragile cause
set in relief, precise as a loved
face.

Insects dwell in the chapel hidden
in sand.

Many years have gone by
until this moment.

C'est la nuit qui parle,
dis-tu.
Mon poème sans mot.
Ma fuite en terre sauvage.

Le corps est léger quand
il est pris pour ce qu'il est.
Composé de murs et de
fenêtres.
Prêt à brûler.
Avec des petits drapeaux
flottant au centre.

Je te caresse avec le secours
du vide.
Une ode à la survie.
Un dictionnaire d'herbes folles.
Pour guérir, nous sommes prêts
à tout.

Night is speaking
you say.
My poem without words.
My flight into wild country.

The body is light when
taken for what it is.
Formed of walls and
windows.
Ready to burn.
With little flags
fluttering   in the center.

I touch you with the help
of the void.
An ode to survival.
A dictionary of wild grasses.
We'll do anything
for a cure.

2004

II

ARCHAIC

Cold wit leaves me cold
this time of the world   Multifoliate disorders
straiten my gait   Minuets don't become me
Been wanting to get out   see the sights
but the exits are slick with people
going somewhere fast
every one with a shared past
and a mot juste   And me so out of step
with my late-night staircase inspirations   my
utopian slant

Still, I'm alive here
in this village drawn in a tightening noose
of ramps and cloverleafs
but the old directions I drew up
for you
are obsolete

Here's how
to get to me
I wrote
Don't misconstrue the distance
take along something for the road
everything might be closed
this isn't a modern place

You arrived starving at midnight
I gave you warmed-up food

poured tumblers of brandy
put on Les Barricades Mystérieuses
—the only jazz in the house
We talked for hours   of barricades
lesser and greater sorrows
ended up laughing in the thicksilver
birdstruck light

2005

LONG AFTER STEVENS

A locomotive pushing through snow in the mountains
more modern than the will

to be modern   The mountain's profile
in undefiled snow disdains

definitions of poetry   It was always
indefinite, task and destruction

the laser eye of the poet   her blind eye
her moment-stricken eye   her unblinking eye

She had to get down from the blocked train
lick snow from bare cupped hands

taste what had soared into that air
—local cinders, steam of the fast machine

clear her palate with a breath   distinguish
through tumbling whiteness   figures

frozen   figures advancing
weapons at the ready
for the new password

She had to feel her tongue
freeze and burn at once

instrument searching, probing
toward a foreign tongue

2005

IMPROVISATION ON LINES
FROM EDWIN MUIR'S
"VARIATIONS ON A TIME THEME"

Packed in my skin from head to toe
Is one I know and do not know

He never speaks to me yet is at home
More snug than embryo in the womb . . .

His name's Indifference
Nothing offending he is all offence . . .

Can note with a lack-lustre eye
Victim and murderer go by . . .

If I could drive this demon out
I'd put all Time's display to rout . . .

Or so I dream when at my door
I hear my Soul, my Visitor.

He comes but seldom, and I cannot tell
If he's myself or one who loves me well
And comes in pity, for he pities all . . .

Victim and murderer . . . Vision's
bloodshot wandering eye engages and

the whetted tool moves toward the hand
scrapes down an impassive sky   debrides

the panicked face   erases or redresses
with understrokes and slashes

in smeared roughed-over surfaces
false moves bad guesses

pausing to gauge its own
guilty innocence, desire

to make it clear yet leave the field
still dark and dialectical

This is unpitying yet not cold

—And Muir I wonder, standing under
the bruised eye-socket of late-winter sun

about your circling double-bind
between indifference and pity

your dream of history as Eden's
loss, all else as repetition

—Wonder at your old opposite
number, Hugh MacDiarmid

his populated outraged joy
his ear for Lenin and for Rilke

for the particular and vast
the thistle's bony elegance

the just, the wild, the urge, the cry for
what must change what be demolished
what secreted for the future

bardic or technological
together dialectical

2005–2006

RHYME

Walking by the fence but the house
   not there

going to the river but the
   river looking spare

bones of the river spread out
   everywhere

O tell me this is home

Crossing the bridge but
   some planks not there

looking at the shore but only
   getting back the glare

dare you trust the river when there's
   no water there

O tell me is this home

Getting into town seeing
   nobody I know

folks standing around
    nowhere to go

staring into the air like
    they saw a show

O tell me was this my home

Come to the railroad no train
    on the tracks

switchman in his shanty
    with a great big axe

so what happened here so what
    are the facts

So tell me where is my home

2005

HOTEL

I dreamed the Finnish Hotel founded by Finns in an olden time
It was in New York had been there a long time
Finnish sea-captains had stayed there in their time
It had fallen on one then another bad time
Now restored it wished to be or seem of the olden time
The Finnish Hotel founded by Finns in an olden time

There was a perpendicular lighted sign along its spine:
THE FINNISH HOTEL and on the desk aligned
two lamps like white globes and a blond
wood lounge with curved chairs and a bar beyond
serving a clear icy liquor of which the captains had been fond
reputedly in the olden time

In the Finnish Hotel I slept on a mattress stuffed with straw
after drinking with a Finnish captain who regarded me with awe
saying, Woman who could put away that much I never saw
but I did not lie with him on the mattress, his major flaw
being he was a phantom of the olden time
and I a woman still almost in my prime

dreaming the Finnish Hotel founded by Finns in the olden time

2005

THREE ELEGIES

i. LATE STYLE

Propped on elbow in stony light
Green lawns of entitlement
out the window you can neither
open nor close

man crouched in den flung trembling
back on failed gifts
lapsed desire   A falling
star   Dim, trapped
in the narrow place of fame

And beneath the skin of boredom
indecipherable fear

ii. AS EVER

As ever, death.   Whenever, where.   But it's
the drawn-together life we're finally
muted by.   Must stand, regard as whole
what was still partial   still
under revision.   So it felt, so we thought.

Then to hear sweep
the scythe on grass
still witherless and sweet

iii. FALLEN FIGURE

The stone walls will recede and the needs that laid them
scar of winter sun stretch low
behind the advancing junipers

darkness rise up from the whitening pond

Crusted silver your breath in this ditch
the pitchfork in your hand
still stuck to your hand

The northern lights
will float, probe, vacillate

the yellow eye
of the snowplow you used to drive
will seek and find you

2005

HUBBLE PHOTOGRAPHS: AFTER SAPPHO

It should be the most desired sight of all
the person with whom you hope to live and die

walking into a room, turning to look at you, sight for sight
Should be yet I say there is something

more desirable: the ex-stasis of galaxies
so out from us there's no vocabulary

but mathematics and optics
equations letting sight pierce through time

into liberations, lacerations of light and dust
exposed like a body's cavity, violet green livid and venous,
    gorgeous

beyond good and evil as ever stained into dream
beyond remorse, disillusion, fear of death

or life, rage
for order, rage for destruction

—beyond this love which stirs
the air every time she walks into the room

These impersonae, however we call them
won't invade us as on movie screens

they are so old, so new, we are not to them
we look at them or don't from within the milky gauze

of our tilted gazing
but they don't look back and we cannot hurt them

for Jack Litewka

2005

THIS IS NOT THE ROOM

of polished tables lit with medalled
torsos bent toward microphones
where ears lean hands scribble
"working the dark side"

—glazed eye meeting frozen eye—

This is not the room where tears down carven
cheeks track rivulets in the scars
left by the gouging tool
where wood itself is weeping

where the ancient painted eye speaks to the living eye

This is the room
where truth scrubs around the pedestal of the toilet
flings her rag into the bucket
straightens up   spits at the mirror

2005

UNKNOWN QUANTITY

Spring nights you pillow your head on a sack
of rich compost   Charcoal, your hair

sheds sparks through your muttered dreams
Deep is your sleep in the starless dark

and you wake in your live skin to show me
a tulip   Not the prizewinning Queen of the Night

furled in her jade wrappings
but the Prince of Darkness, the not-yet, the X

crouched in his pale bulb
held out in the palm of your hand

Shall we bury him wait and see what happens
will there be time for waiting and to see

2005

TACTILE VALUE

from crush and splinter
death in the market

jeering robotic
dry-ice disrupt

to conjure this:
perishing
persistent script

scratched-up smeared
and torn

> *let hair, nail cuttings*
> *nourish the vine and fig tree*

> *let man, woman*
> *eat, be sheltered*

. . .

Marx the physician laid his ear
on the arhythmic heart

felt the belly
diagnosed the pain

did not precisely write
of lips roaming damp skin

54

hand plunged in hair   bed-laughter
mouth clasping mouth

> *(what we light with this coalspark*
> *living instantly in us*
> *if it continue*

2005–2006

MIDNIGHT, THE SAME DAY

i

When the sun seals my eyes the emblem
of failure will still be standing
motionless at this intersection
between family restaurant
and medical clinic
wearing his cardboard necklace lettered
H ARD LU CK

until his sister
the Fury of reparations
descends
curdling the air in whirlwind
tears it from his neck
picks him up and hurls on

ii

Try to rest now, says a voice.
Another: *Give yourself time.*
But rest is no act of will
and gifts to the self come back unopened
Milk will boil down in the iron pot
blistering into black sugar,
scalded vinegar lift
crispened layers
pages of a codex
in a library blown away

2005

EVEN THEN MAYBE

Not spent   those bloodshot friendships   those
soul-marriages sealed and torn
those smiles of pain
I told her a mouthful
I shut my mouth against him
Throat thick with tears
how words sound when you swallow
—and under the roof
of the mouth   long stroke
reaching from the tongue's root

No, I was not living with her at the time
At the time I was not living
with him, at the time we were living together
I was living with neither of them
—was dwelling you could say
But as for living at that time
we were all living together with many others
for whom living was precisely the question

Haven't seen evenings like that since
vesuvian emerald to brass dissolving
—a sentence you'd waited for
taken back half-spoken—
Luxury even then maybe
evenings like those

2005

DIRECTOR'S NOTES

You don't want a harsh outcry here
not to violate the beauty yet
dawn unveiling ochre village
but to show coercion
within that beauty, endurance required
Begin with girl
pulling hand over hand on chain
only sound drag and creak
in time it becomes monotonous

then must begin sense of unease produced by monotony
repetitive motion, repetitive sound
resistance, irritation
increasing for the viewers
sense of what are they here for, anyway
dislike of the whole thing how boring to watch

(they aren't used to duration
this was a test)

Keep that dislike that boredom as a value
also as risk
so when bucket finally tinks at rim
they breathe a sigh, not so much relief
as finally grasping
what all this was for

dissolve as she dips from bucket

2005

REREADING *THE DEAD LECTURER*

Overthrow.   And make new.

An idea.   And we felt it.
A meaning.   And we caught it
as the dimensions spread, gathering
in pre-utopian basements   figured shadows
scrawled with smoke and music.
                              Shed the dead hand,
let sound be sense.   A world
echoing everywhere, Fanon, Freire, thin pamphlets lining
raincoat pockets, poetry on walls, damp purple mimeos cranking
—the feeling of an idea.   An idea of feeling.

That love could be so resolute

And the past?   Overthrow of systems, forms
could not overthrow the past
                              nor our
                                        neglect of consequences.
Nor that cold will we misnamed.

There were consequences.   A world
repeating everywhere: the obliterations.
What's surreal, hyperreal, virtual,
what's poetry what's verse what's new.   What is

a political art.   If we
(who?) ever were conned
into mere definitions.

                 If we

                      accept

(book of a soul contending

2005

III

LETTERS CENSORED
SHREDDED
RETURNED TO SENDER
OR JUDGED UNFIT TO SEND

Unless in quotation marks (for which see Notes on the Poems), the letter fragments are written by various imaginary persons.

"We must prevent this mind from functioning . . .": words of the prosecutor sentencing Antonio Gramsci to prison, June 2, 1928.

—Could you see me laboring over this
right arm in sling, typing left-handed with one finger—

{On a scale of one to ten what is your pain today}

〜

—shall I measure the split atoms
of pleasure flying outward from the core—

〜

—To think of her naked every day unfreezes me—

〜

Banditry, rapes, burning the woods
"a kind of primitive class struggle
with no lasting or effective results"

—The bakers strike, the needleworkers strike, the mechanics strike, the miners strike

the great machine coughs out the pieces and hurtles on—

〰

—then there are days all thought comes down to sound:
Rust. August. Mattress. Must.
Chains...

—when consciousness + sensation feels like/ = suffering—

〰

—the people, yes, as yet unformed—deformed—no: disinformed—

〰

—What's realistic fantasy?—Call it hope—

〰

—heard your voice on the news tonight, its minor key
your old-fashioned mindfulness—could have loved you again—

〰

—Autumn invades my body, anger
wrapped in forgiving sunlight, fear of the cold—

〰

—Words gather like flies above this carcass of meaning—

~~

"this void, this vacuum"

~~

—You think you are helpless because you are empty-handed
of concepts that could become your strength—

~~

—we're told it's almost over, but we see no sign of it yet—

~~

"caught between a feeling of immense tenderness for you
which seems . . . a weakness
that could only be consoled
by an immediate physical caress . . ."

[*We must prevent this mind from functioning for twenty years*]

". . . and these inadequate, cold and colorless words"

~~

—What I meant to write, belov'd critic, then struck it out
thinking you might accuse me of
whatever you would:
I wanted a sensual materialism to utter pleasure

Something beyond a cry that could sound like a groan—

~~~

—Vocalizing forbidden syllables—

~~~

—our mythologies choke us, we have enthralled ourselves—

~~~

> [*Writing like this for the censors*
> *but I won't hide behind words*]

~~~

"my body cells revolve in unison
with the whole universe

> The cycle of the seasons, the progression of the solstices
> and equinoxes
> I feel them as flesh of my flesh
> and under the snow the first violets are already trembling
> > In short, time has seemed to me a thing of flesh
> > ever since space
> > ceased to exist for me"

~~~

—History = bodies in time—

or, in your language:

$$H = \frac{T}{b}$$

—to think of the one asleep
in that field beside the chimney
of the burnt-out house
a thing of flesh, exhausted—

—this flash is all we know . . . . can we shut our eyes to it . . . ?—

—more and more I dread futility—

"The struggle, whose normal external expressions
have been choked,
attaches itself to the structure
of the old class like a destructive gangrene . . .
it takes on morbid forms of mysticism,
sensualism, moral indifference,
physical and psychic pathological depravations . . .
The old structure does not contain and is unable
to satisfy the new needs . . ."

—Trying to hold an inner focus while hoarse laughter
ricochets from the guardroom—

～

—*liquefaction* is a word I might use for how I would take you—

～

—the daunted river finally
undammed?—

[*prevent this mind*]

2005

IV

IF/AS THOUGH

you'd spin out on your pirate platter
chords I'd receive on my crystal set
blues purpling burgundy goblets
Lorca's piano spuming up champagne flutes
could drop over any night at will
with that bottle of Oregon Pinot to watch *Alexander Nevsky*
If no curfews no blackouts no
no-fly lists no profiling racial genital mental
If all necessary illicits blew in
like time-release capsules or spores in the mulch
up-rising as morels, creviced and wild-delicious   If
Gerard Manley Hopkins were here to make welsh rarebit
reciting *The Wreck of the Deutschland* to Hart Crane in his high tenor
guessing him captive audience to sprung rhythm   as we in lóst lóve
sequences   hearing it
                    skim uncurfewed, uncowled
pelicans over spindrift beating agnostic wings

for Ed Pavlić

2006

TIME EXPOSURES

i

Glance into glittering moisture
webbed in lashes   unshed tears
I'd guess as yours
Known odor inhaled years later
in a brief social kiss   sudden conjuncture
soap, sweat, breath, hair   other embraces
diffused   once, again, time's exhilarations

ii

Is there a doctor in the house
who in his plain mindful way
cared for his patients through
pain rain and snow

who at each and every grave
side knew
what could be done
he'd done

And where have all the patients gone
who wanted (more than one)
a tending hand
across the forehead   at the end

And what's the house?

iii

They'd say she was humorless
didn't go to the parties
giggle   show white teeth

So would suspend her in
their drained
definitions

Her body had nipples, eyes
a tongue and other parts

mirthful
obscene

which rose from love   quite often
hilarious into daylight
even forgetting why

iv

When I stretched out my legs beyond your wishful thinking
into the long history they were made for running
caught the train you missed sought you eye-level
at the next station You having run the whole way
to seize my face between your hands your kind
of victory or benediction then
we swerved down-tunnel
in separate cars What is it to
catch yourself mirror-twinned
in an underwater window what
about speed matching
technology and desire getting off
at the last stop: dispersed

v

You've got ocean through sheet glass brandy and firelog
ocean in its shaking
looks back at you with a blurred eye

Who's that reflected
naked and sundered

reaching a hand

Go
down to the beach, walk in the wind
Pick up the washed-in shell
at your foot

Shell castle built on sand
your body and what's your soul?

Is there a ghost-in-waiting?
time to bring that one in

2006

THE UNIVERSITY REOPENS
AS THE FLOODS RECEDE

Should blue air in its purity let you disdain
the stink of artificial pine

the gaunt architecture
of cheap political solutions

if there are philosophies to argue
the moment when you would

or wouldn't spring to shield
a friend's body or jump

into scummed waters after
a stranger caught submerging

or walk off to your parked
car your sandwich your possible orange

if theories rage or dance
about this if in the event   any

can be sure who did
or did not act on principle or impulse

and what's most virtuous

can we not be nodding smiling
taking down notes like this

and of all places
in a place like this

I'll work with you on this bad matter   I can
but won't give you the time of day

if you think it's hypothetical

2006

VIA INSOMNIA

Called up in sleep: your voice:
I don't know where I am . . .

A hand, mine, stroking a white fur surface
you as a white fur hat unstitched, outspread

white as your cold brancusian marble head
what animal's pelt resembles you?
but these are my navigations: *you don't know where you are*

Is this how it is to be newly dead?   unbelieving
the personal soul, electricity unsheathing
from the cortex, light-waves fleeing
into the black universe

to lie awake half-sleeping, wondering
Where, when will I sleep

for Tory Dent

2006

A BURNING KANGAROO

leaping forward   escaping
out of rock reamed
on sky
in violet shadow

leaping   scorched to the skin

toward water
(none for miles)

Who did
            (and can you see
this thing
            not as a dream

a kangaroo
and not in profile either

Frontal
in flame   no halo
no aura   burning meat in movement

Can
you see with me
                (unverified
otherwise

(whoever   did this thing

2006

82

EVER, AGAIN

Mockingbird shouts *Escape! Escape!*
and would I could   I'd

fly, drive back to that house
up the long hill between queen

anne's lace and common daisyface
shoulder open stuck door

run springwater from kitchen
tap   drench tongue

palate and throat
throw window sashes up screens down

breathe in   mown grass
pine-needle heat

manure, lilac   unpack
brown sacks from the store:

ground meat, buns, tomatoes, one
big onion, milk and orange juice

iceberg lettuce, ranch dressing
potato chips, dill pickles

the *Caledonian-Record*
Portuguese rosé in round-hipped flask

open the box of newspapers by the stove
reread: (Vietnam Vietnam)

Set again on the table
the Olivetti, the stack

of rough yellow typing paper
mark the crashed instant

of one summer's mosquito
on a bedroom door

voices of boys outside
proclaiming twilight and hunger

Pour iced vodka into a shotglass
get food on the table

sitting with those wild heads
over hamburgers, fireflies, music

staying up late with the typewriter
falling asleep with the dead

2006

V

DRAFT #2006

i

Suppose we came back as ghosts asking the unasked questions.

(What were you there for? Why did you walk out? What would have made you stay? Why wouldn't you listen?)

—Couldn't you show us what you meant, can't we get it right this time? Can't you put it another way?—

(You were looking for openings where they'd been walled up—)

—But you were supposed to be our teacher—

(One-armed, I was trying to get you, one by one, out of that cellar. It wasn't enough)

ii

Dreamfaces blurring horrorlands: border of poetry.

Ebb tide sucks out clinging rockpool creatures, no swimming
back into sleep.

Clockface says too early, body prideful and humble shambles
into another day, reclaiming itself piecemeal in private ritual
acts.

Reassembling the anagram scattered nightly, rebuilding daily
the sand city.

iii

What's concrete for me: from there I cast out further.

But need to be there. On the stone causeway. Baffled and obstinate.

Eyes probing the dusk. Foot-slippage possible.

iv

Sleeping that time at the philosopher's house.   Not lovers,
friends from the past.

Music the vertex of our triangle.   Bach our hypotenuse
strung between philosophy and poetry.

Sun loosening fog on the hillside, cantata spun on the
turntable: *Wie schön leuchtet der Morgenstern.*

Feeling again, in our mid-forties, the old contrapuntal ten-
sion between our natures.   The future as if still open, like
when we were classmates.

He'd met Heidegger in the Black Forest, corresponded
with Foucault.   We talked about Wittgenstein.

I was on my way to meet the one who said *Philosophers have
interpreted the world: the point is to change it.*

v

On a street known for beautiful shops she buys a piece of
antique Japanese silk, a white porcelain egg.

Had abandoned her child, later went after him, found the
child had run away.

Hurt and angry, joined a group to chant through the pain.
They said, you must love yourself, give yourself gifts.

Whatever eases you someone says, lets you forgive yourself,
let go.

America, someone says.

Orphaning, orphaned here, don't even know it.

vi

Silent limousines meet jets descending over the Rockies.
Steam rooms, pure thick towels, vases of tuberose and jas-
mine, old vintages await the après-skiers.

Rooms of mahogany and leather, conversations open in
international code.   Thighs and buttocks to open later by
arrangement.

Out of sight, out of mind, she solitary wrestles a huge
duvet, resheathes heavy tasselled bolsters.   Bed after bed.
Nights, in her room, ices strained arms.   Rests her legs.

Elsewhere, in Andhra Pradesh, another farmer swallows
pesticide.

vii

Condemned, a clinic coughs up its detritus.

Emergency exit, gurneys lined double, mercy draining
down exhausted tubes.

Drills and cranes clearing way for the new premises.

As if I already stood at their unglazed windows, eyeing the
distressed site through skeletal angles.

Tenant already of the disensoulment projects.

Had thought I deserved nothing better than these stark
towers named for conglomerates?—a line of credit, a give-
away?

viii

They asked me, is this time worse than another.

I said, for whom?

Wanted to show them something.   While I wrote on the chalkboard they drifted out. I turned back to an empty room.

Maybe I couldn't write fast enough.   Maybe it was too soon.

ix

The sheer mass of the thing, its thereness, stuns thought.
Since it exists, it must have existed.   Will exist.   It says so
here.

Excruciating contempt for love.   For the strained fibre of
common affections, mutual assistance

sifted up from landfill, closed tunnels, drought-sheared
riverbeds, street beds named in old census books, choked
under the expressway.

Teachers bricolating scattered schools of trust.   Rootlets
watered by fugitives.

Contraband packets, hummed messages.   Dreams of the
descendants, surfacing.

Hand reaching for its like exposes a scarred wrist.
Numerals.   A bracelet of rust.

In a desert observatory, under plaster dust, smashed lenses
left by the bombardments,

star maps crackle, unscrolling.

2006

VI

TELEPHONE RINGING IN THE LABYRINTH

i

You who can be silent in twelve languages
trying to crease again in paling light
the map you unfurled that morning   if

you in your rearview mirror sighted me
rinsing a green glass bowl
by midsummer nightsun in, say, Reykjavík

if at that moment my hand slipped
and that bowl cracked to pieces
and one piece stared at me like a gibbous moon

if its convex reflection caught you walking
the slurried highway shoulder after the car broke down
if such refractions matter

ii

Well, I've held on   peninsula
to continent, climber
to rockface

Sensual peninsula attached so   stroked
by the tides' pensive and moody hands
Scaler into thin air

seen from below as weed or lichen
improvidently fastened
a mat of hair webbed in a bush

A bush ignited   then
consumed
Violent lithography

smolder's legacy on a boulder traced

iii

Image erupts from image
atlas from vagrancy
articulation from mammal howl

strangeness from repetition
even this   default location
surveyed again   one more poem

one more Troy or Tyre or burning tire
seared eyeball genitals
charred cradle

but a different turn   working
this passage of the labyrinth
as laboratory

I'd have entered, searched before
but that ball of thread   that clew
offering an exit choice was no gift at all

iv

I found you by design or
was it your design
or: we were drawn, we drew

Midway in this delicate
negotiation   telephone rings
(Don't stop! . . . they'll call again . . .)

Offstage the fabulous creature scrapes and shuffles
we breathe its heavy dander
I don't care how, if it dies   this is not the myth

No ex/interior: compressed
between my throat
and yours, hilarious oxygen

And, for the record, each did sign
our true names on the register
at the mouth of this hotel

v

I would have wanted to say it
without falling back
on words   Desired not

you so much as your life,
your prevailing   Not for me
but for furtherance   how

you would move
on the horizon   You, the person, you
the particle   fierce and furthering

2006

NOTES
ON
THE POEMS

From Alan Davies, review of Brenda Iijima's *Around Sea* (Oakland, Calif.: O Books, 2004), in *St. Mark's in the Bowery Poetry Newsletter* (April/May 2004), used by permission of Alan Davies; and from Michael S. Harper, *Songlines in Michaeltree: New and Collected Poems* (Urbana: University of Illinois Press, 2000).

Landstuhl: American military hospital in Germany.
"You go to war with the army you have"; U.S. Secretary of Defense Donald Rumsfeld, December 2004.

MELANCHOLY PIANO (extracts)

This translation was published as part of an international poetry project by the Quebec literary magazine *Estuaire* and the *New Review of Literature* (Otis College of Art and Design, Los Angeles) with Quebecois and Anglophone-American poets translating poems by their counterparts.

Élise Turcotte's works include *Sombre Ménagerie* (Montreal: Éditions du Noroît, 2002) and *Diligence* (Longueuil: Les Petits Villages, 2004). Her novel *The Alien House* (Toronto: Cormorant Books, 2004) translated into English by Sheila Fischman, received the Canadian Governor General's Prize.

Improvisation on Lines from Edwin Muir's "Variations on a Time Theme"

See Edwin Muir, *Collected Poems, 1921–1951* (London: Faber and Faber, 1952), and John C. Weston, ed., *Collected Poems of Hugh MacDiarmid*, rev. ed. (New York: Macmillan, 1967).

Hubble Photographs: After Sappho

For Sappho, see *Greek Lyric*, I: *Sappho, Alcaeus,* trans. David A. Campbell, Loeb Classical Library 142 (Cambridge, Mass.: Harvard University Press, 1982–), fragment 16, pp. 66–67: "Some say a host of cavalry, others of infantry, and others of ships, is the most beautiful thing on the black earth, but I say it is whatsoever a person loves. . . . I would rather see her lovely walk and the bright sparkle of her face than the Lydians' chariots and armed infantry."

This Is Not the Room

U.S. Vice President Richard Cheney, on NBC's *Meet the Press*, September 16, 2001: "we also have to work, though, sort of, the dark side . . . use any means at our disposal, basically, to achieve our objective."

Rereading *The Dead Lecturer*

See LeRoi Jones (Amiri Baraka), *The Dead Lecturer: Poems* (New York: Grove, 1967).

Letters Censored, Shredded, Returned to Sender, or Judged Unfit to Send

Passages in quotes are from Giuseppe Fiori, *Antonio Gramsci: Life of a Revolutionary*, trans. Tom Nairn (New York: Verso, 1990), pp. 31, 239; Antonio Gramsci, *Prison Letters*, ed. and trans. Hamish Henderson (London: Pluto Press, 1996), p. 135; and *Antonio Gramsci, Prison Notebooks,* ed. Joseph A. Buttigeig, trans. Joseph A. Buttigeig and Antonio Callari, 2 vols. (New York: Columbia University Press, 1992), I, p. 213.

Draft #2006

vi: *Out of sight, out of mind*: See Carolyn Jones, "Battle of the Beds," *San Francisco Chronicle*, December 19, 2005, p. A-1.

ACKNOWLEDGMENTS

My thanks to the editors of journals in which these poems first appeared, some in earlier versions:

American Poetry Review: "Via Insomnia," "Rhyme," "Wallpaper," "Time Exposures"

Bloom: "Hubble Photographs: After Sappho," "Midnight, the Same Day" (as "Sign")

Monthly Review: An Independant Socialist Magazine: "Director's Notes"

MR webzine: http://mrzine.monthlyreview.org: "Tactile Value" (as "A Debt to the World")

The Nation: "Even Then Maybe"

The New Review of Literature: "Long after Stevens," "Melancholy Piano"

The Progressive: "This Is Not the Room"

The Virginia Quarterly Review: "Archaic," "Behind the Motel," "Calibrations," "In Plain Sight," "Rereading *The Dead Lecturer*," "Skeleton Key, "Voyage to the Dénouement," "Unknown Quantity"

Xcp: Cross Cultural Poetics: "Letters Censored, Shredded, Returned to Sender, or Judged Unfit to Send," "Telephone Ringing in the Labyrinth," "The University Reopens as the Floods Recede"

Mandorla: Nuevas Escrituras de las Américas/New Writing from the Americas published the following in Spanish: "Archaic," "Rereading *The Dead Lecturer*," "Skeleton Key."

Mita'am: A Review of Literature and Radical Thought (Israel) published "Even Then Maybe" and "This Is Not the Room" in Hebrew.

I thank my editor, Jill Bialosky, and her colleagues at W. W. Norton in New York and London; our working relationship is now a story of many years

and for their principled dedication: Frances Goldin, Steven Barclay, and their associates

and for many kinds of talk and work over the years: Svetlana Alpers; Chantal Bizzini; David, Pablo, and Jacob Conrad; Clayton Eshleman; Suzanne Gardinier; Albert and Barbara Gelpi; Peter Gizzi; Jack Litewka; Mark Nowak; Ed Pavlić; James Scully; Hugh Seidman; Marisol Soledad Sánchez; Helen Smelser; Jean Valentine; Maria Luisa Vezzali; Elizabeth Willis

and, once again, for her words, for a life: Michelle Cliff